A Coloring about

JESUS

Words and Pictures
By Emma C. Mc Kean

CATHOLIC BOOK PUBLISHING CORP.
New Jersey

Jesus calms the great storm.

T-670

NIHIL OBSTAT: Daniel V. Flynn, J.C.D., *Censor Librorum*
IMPRIMATUR: Joseph T. O'Keefe, *Vicar General, Archdiocese of New York*

Jesus feeds the hungry.

3

Jesus with John the Baptist.

Jesus walks on the water.

Jesus changes water into wine.

**Jesus teaches the people to pray
to our Father in Heaven.**

Jesus shines brightly in a white heavenly light,
when He goes up a mountain with Peter,
James, and John.

**Jesus teaches religion to Martha and
Mary, the sisters of Lazarus.**

Jesus speaks to Zacchaeus, the little man who is looking for salvation, and finds it.

Jesus washes the feet of the apostles to teach us to care for others.

Jesus heals the sick.

Jesus blesses the poor.

One day Jesus met a man who said, "Lord, I am
not worthy that You should come to my house,
but only say the word, and my servant shall be
14 healed."

Now at Mass, we say, "Lord, I am not worthy that You should come to me, but only say the word, and I shall be healed."

I THINK about JESUS

I often think about Our Lord and Savior Jesus Christ.
I believe that He cares about me very much.

I love to think that Jesus is always near me.

Help me to be like You.

Thank You.

Dear Jesus, You are All-Good and kind.

I love to think that Jesus is always near me.

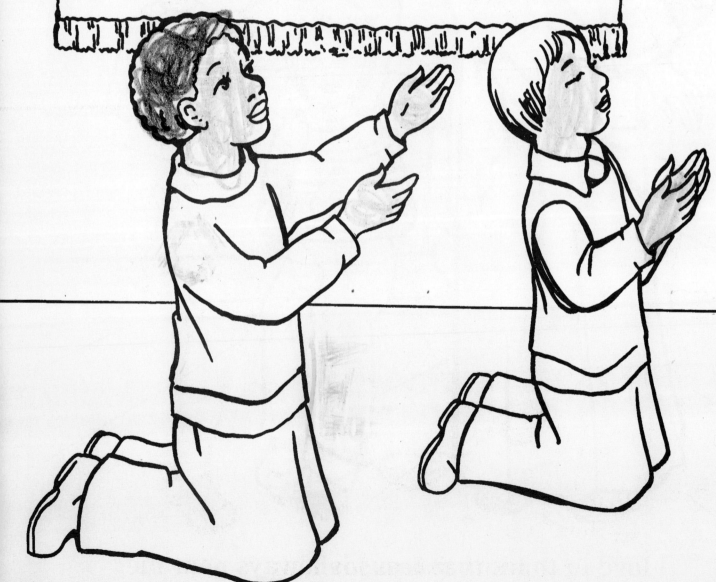

JESUS is MY BEST FRIEND

18

PEACE

Jesus listens lovingly.

JESUS
IS THE
BREAD
OF
LIFE

See how neatly you can color this poster. Be careful not to get any color in the white circle.

20

At the Last Supper, Jesus gives us the Sacrament of the Holy Eucharist.

21

"Hosanna in the Highest. . . .

Blessed is He Who comes in the Name of the Lord."

**Jesus said to Thomas:
"Blessed are those who have not seen,
yet have believed."**

**Jesus teaches us how very important it is
for us to believe.**

Jesus said, "Let the little children come to Me..."

Jesus loves little children and gives them His blessings.

Jesus is the Good Shepherd.

Jesus watches over us with loving care.

Before Jesus goes back to heaven. He tells His apostles to go forth and baptize people of all nations.

30

Jesus tells Peter,
"Feed My sheep.
Take care of My lambs."

31

Jesus will come again.